World Lar.

# Colors in English

## Daniel Nunn

Chicago, Illinois

**www.capstonepub.com**
Visit our website to find out more information about Heinemann-Raintree books.

**To order:**

☎ Phone 800-747-4992
💻 Visit www.capstonepub.com to browse our catalog and order online.

Edited by Rebecca Rissman, Dan Nunn,
   and Sian Smith
Designed by Joanna Hinton-Malivoire
Picture research by Elizabeth Alexander
Production by Alison Parsons
Originated by Capstone Global Library Ltd
Printed and bound in China by South China Printing Company Ltd

16 15 14 13 12
10 9 8 7 6 5 4 3 2 1

**Library of Congress Cataloging-in-Publication Data**
Nunn, Daniel.
  Colors in English / Daniel Nunn.
     p. cm.—(World languages - Colors)
  Includes bibliographical references and index.
ISBN 978-1-4329-6656-0 (hbk.)—ISBN 978-1-4329-6663-8 (pbk.)
1. English language—Textbooks for foreign speakers—Juvenile literature. 2. Colors—Juvenile literature. I. Title.
  PE1128.N86 2013
  428.1—dc23                    2011046690

**Acknowledgments**
We would like to thank Shutterstock for permission to reproduce photographs: pp.4 (© Phiseksit), 5 (© Stephen Aaron Rees), 6, 23 (© Tischenko Irina), 7 (© Tony Magdaraog), 8 (© szefei), 9 (© Picsfive), 10 (© Eric Isselée), 11 (© Yasonya), 12, 23 (© Nadezhda Bolotina), 13 (© Maryna Gviazdovska), 14, 23 (© Erik Lam), 15 (© Eric Isselée), 16, 22 (© Ruth Black), 17 (© blueskies9), 18, 22 (© Alexander Dashewsky), 19 (© Michele Perbellini), 20, 22 (© Eric Isselée), 21 (© Roman Rvachov).

Cover photographs reproduced with permission of Shutterstock: dog (© Erik Lam), strawberry (© Stephen Aaron Rees), fish (© Tischenko Irina). Back cover photograph of an apple reproduced with permission of Shutterstock (© Yasonya).

Every effort has been made to contact copyright holders of material reproduced in this book. Any omissions will be rectified in subsequent printings if notice is given to the publisher.

# Contents

# Red

book

The book is red.

strawberry

The strawberry is red.

# Orange

fish

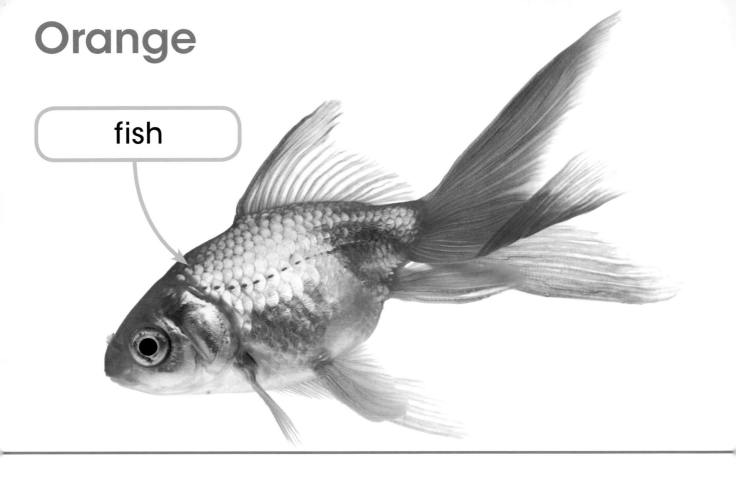

The fish is orange.

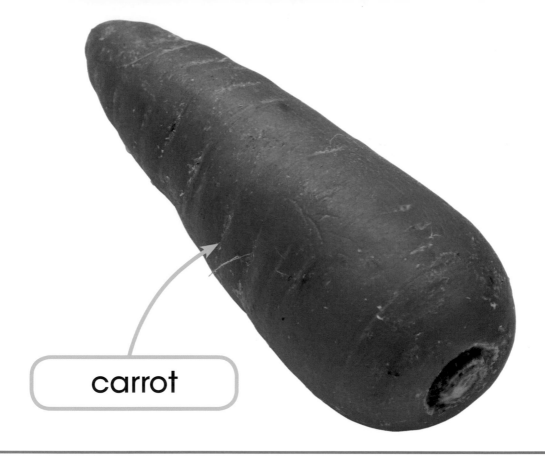

carrot

The carrot is orange.

# Yellow

flower

The flower is yellow.

banana

The banana is yellow.

# Green

bird

The bird is green.

apple

The apple is green.

# Blue

T-shirt

The T-shirt is blue.

cup

The cup is blue.

# Brown

dog

The dog is brown.

COW

The cow is brown.

# Pink

cake

The cake is pink.

hat

The hat is pink.

# White

milk

The milk is white.

snow

The snow is white.

# Black

The cat is **black**.

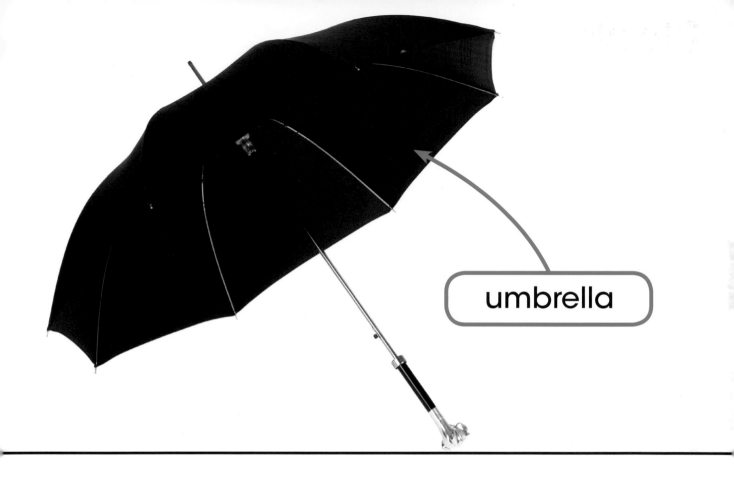

umbrella

The umbrella is **black**.

# Can You Remember?

What color was the milk?

What color was the cat?

What color was the cake?

What color was the fish?

What color was the dog?

What color was the T-shirt?

Answers on page 24

| | |
|---|---|
| black 20, 21 | pink 16, 17 |
| blue 12, 13 | red 4, 5 |
| brown 14, 15 | white 18, 19 |
| green 10, 11 | yellow 8, 9 |
| orange 6, 7 | |

**Answers to questions on pages 22 and 23**

The milk was white.
The cat was black.
The cake was pink.
The fish was orange.
The dog was brown.
The T-shirt was blue.